LEO

THE SURVIVORS

EPISODE 4

QUANTUM ANOMALIES

CINEBOOK
The 9th Art Publisher

PREVIOUSLY

A spaceship bound for Aldebaran was destroyed in an accident. A handful of survivors found themselves on an unknown planet; some among them experienced a time distortion event caused by the quantum anomalies that randomly strike the planet's surface. For Marie, Alex, Ilse and Max, only a few days passed, whereas for the rest of the group, six long years went by in the company of the Holorans – benevolent aliens who looked like Earth felines. The quantum anomalies seemed to be more concentrated in a specific spot. To determine why, an expedition was launched, but it was soon attacked by a group of violent, squid-like aliens. Djamila was kidnapped and held captive while Marie and Alex were forced by their abductors to enter a time distortion zone. Their Holoran friends Antac and Selkert flew their plane into the zone to help them. All four of them would inevitably suffer a temporal jump. But by how many days, months or years would they have moved forward this time?…

Original title: Episode 4
Original edition: © Dargaud Paris 2016 by Leo
www.dargaud.com
All rights reserved
English translation: © 2017 Cinebook Ltd
Translator: Jerome Saincantin
Editor: Erica Olson Jeffrey
Lettering and text layout: Design Amorandi
Printed in Spain by EGEDSA
This edition first published in Great Britain in 2017 by
Cinebook Ltd
56 Beech Avenue
Canterbury, Kent
CT4 7TA
www.cinebook.com
A CIP catalogue record for this book
is available from the British Library
ISBN 978-1-84918-346-8

9th CINEBOOK
The 9th Art Publisher

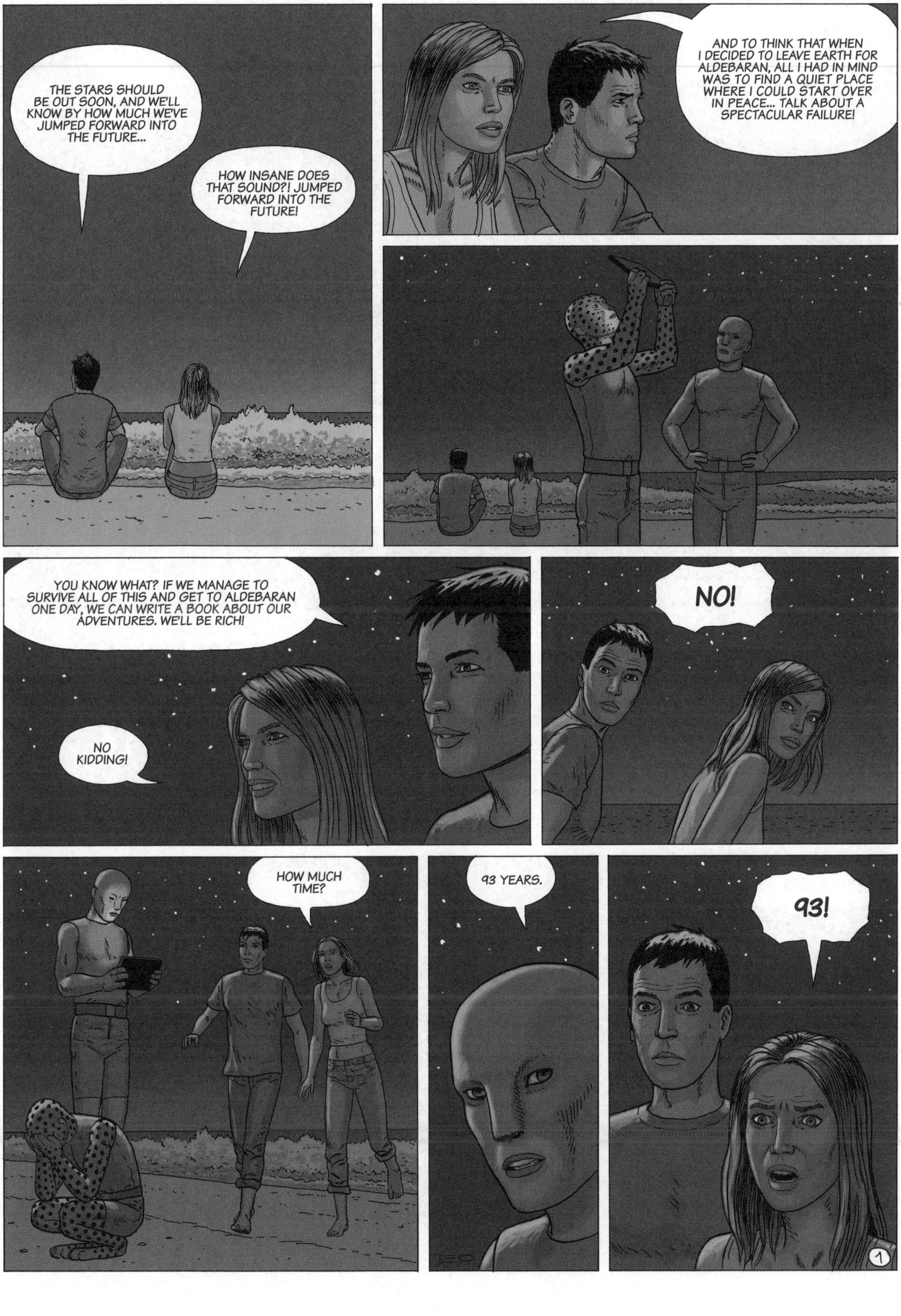
THE STARS SHOULD BE OUT SOON, AND WE'LL KNOW BY HOW MUCH WE'VE JUMPED FORWARD INTO THE FUTURE...
HOW INSANE DOES THAT SOUND?! JUMPED FORWARD INTO THE FUTURE!
AND TO THINK THAT WHEN I DECIDED TO LEAVE EARTH FOR ALDEBARAN, ALL I HAD IN MIND WAS TO FIND A QUIET PLACE WHERE I COULD START OVER IN PEACE... TALK ABOUT A SPECTACULAR FAILURE!
YOU KNOW WHAT? IF WE MANAGE TO SURVIVE ALL OF THIS AND GET TO ALDEBARAN ONE DAY, WE CAN WRITE A BOOK ABOUT OUR ADVENTURES. WE'LL BE RICH!
NO KIDDING!
NO!
HOW MUCH TIME?
93 YEARS.
93!
LEO
1

'ALMOST A CENTURY! THAT MEANT ALL OUR FRIENDS WERE GONE. ILSE WAS GONE, AND SO WAS MY MOTHER ON EARTH!...'

'SELKERT SEEMED FURIOUS. SHE AND ANTAC BEGAN ARGUING IN THEIR LANGUAGE. NEITHER MARIE NOR I DARED MAKE A SOUND.'

COME ON. LET'S GO HOME. WE'RE LEAVING IMMEDIATELY.

IT'S JUST THE TWO OF US NOW. WE'RE THE ONLY HUMANS LEFT ON THIS PLANET.

A FEW MINUTES LATER...

OVER THERE! LOOK!

IT'S THAT FLOATING VILLAGE! DJAMILA'S KIDNAPPERS!

IF THEY'RE STILL HERE, THAT MEANS THEY UNDERWENT THE TEMPORAL LEAP TOO!

②

YES! AND THAT MEANS WE CAN GO AND FREE DJAMILA!

EXACTLY!

I'M TURNING AROUND. WE NEED TO COME UP WITH AN ATTACK PLAN.

I CAN ONLY THINK OF ONE WAY: USE THE PLANE TO CAUSE A FIRE AND CREATE A DIVERSION. THAT WAY WE'LL HAVE AN EASIER TIME SNEAKING INTO THEIR VILLAGE.

YES, I AGREE.

YOU MEAN DESTROY THE PLANE?!

HOW WOULD WE LEAVE AFTERWARDS, THEN? AND HOW WOULD WE GET HOME?

THAT'S IRRELEVANT. WHAT MATTERS IS FREEING DJAMILA AND SHOWING HER KIDNAPPERS THAT NO ONE CAN MESS WITH THE HOLORANS WITHOUT SUFFERING THE CONSEQUENCES.

WE'LL HAVE TO IMPROVISE A WAY TO ESCAPE. AS FOR THE RETURN HOME, THAT'S A PROBLEM WE'LL SOLVE LATER. FOR THE MOMENT, THE MAIN THING IS TO RESCUE DJAMILA.

'I WAS ASTONISHED BY ANTAC'S ALL-OR-NOTHING PLAN. I THOUGHT IT WAS ACTUALLY SUICIDAL!'

I'LL TAKE YOU BACK TO THE ISLAND WHERE WE CAMPED. YOU DON'T HAVE THE NECESSARY TRAINING TO GO ON SUCH A MISSION.

WHAT? NO, ABSOLUTELY NOT! I WANT TO GO WITH YOU!

3

I DON'T THINK YOU UNDERSTAND, MARIE. TO FIND AND RESCUE DJAMILA, WE'RE GOING TO HAVE TO PULL OUT ALL THE STOPS AND FACE DOZENS OF ENEMIES IN CLOSE-QUARTERS COMBAT.

ANTAC AND I ARE SOLDIERS, TRAINED FOR BATTLE. YOU'RE NOT. NOT TO MENTION THAT YOU'RE TOO WEAK PHYSICALLY. YOU WON'T LAST FIVE MINUTES!

'SELKERT'S ARGUMENTS SOUNDED SELF-EVIDENT TO ME. BUT NOT TO MARIE...'

NO! I INSIST ON GOING WITH YOU! I KNOW HOW TO FIGHT! YOU'RE GOING TO RESCUE A HUMAN LIKE ME — DJAMILA ISN'T HOLORAN. I HAVE A MORAL OBLIGATION TO HELP YOU!

'OH, MARIE AND HER MORAL OBLIGATIONS! I WAS JUST ABOUT TO SAY THAT I DISAGREED WITH HER, BUT I NEVER GOT THE CHANCE...'

ALL RIGHT. FINE, BUT ON ONE CONDITION: ONCE WE GET THERE, YOU'LL BE ON YOUR OWN. DON'T COUNT ON US TO PROTECT YOU!

I SUPPOSE YOU'RE OF THE SAME MIND AS MARIE...

ER... YES, YES, OF COURSE!...

'HOW COULD I HAVE SAID OTHERWISE? HOW COULD I EVEN THINK OF LETTING MARIE GO ON HER OWN? ONCE AGAIN, IT HAD NOTHING TO DO WITH ACTUAL COURAGE — I SIMPLY DIDN'T HAVE A CHOICE!'

I'M GOING TO TOUCH DOWN WITH THE PLANE POINTING AT ONE OF THE LARGEST BUILDINGS. WE'LL JUMP INTO THE WATER AT THE LAST SECOND. WHEN THE PLANE TOUCHES THE STRUCTURE, THAT SMALL GRENADE THAT SELKERT IS RIGGING ONTO THE ETHANOL TANK WILL CAUSE A BIG EXPLOSION.

④

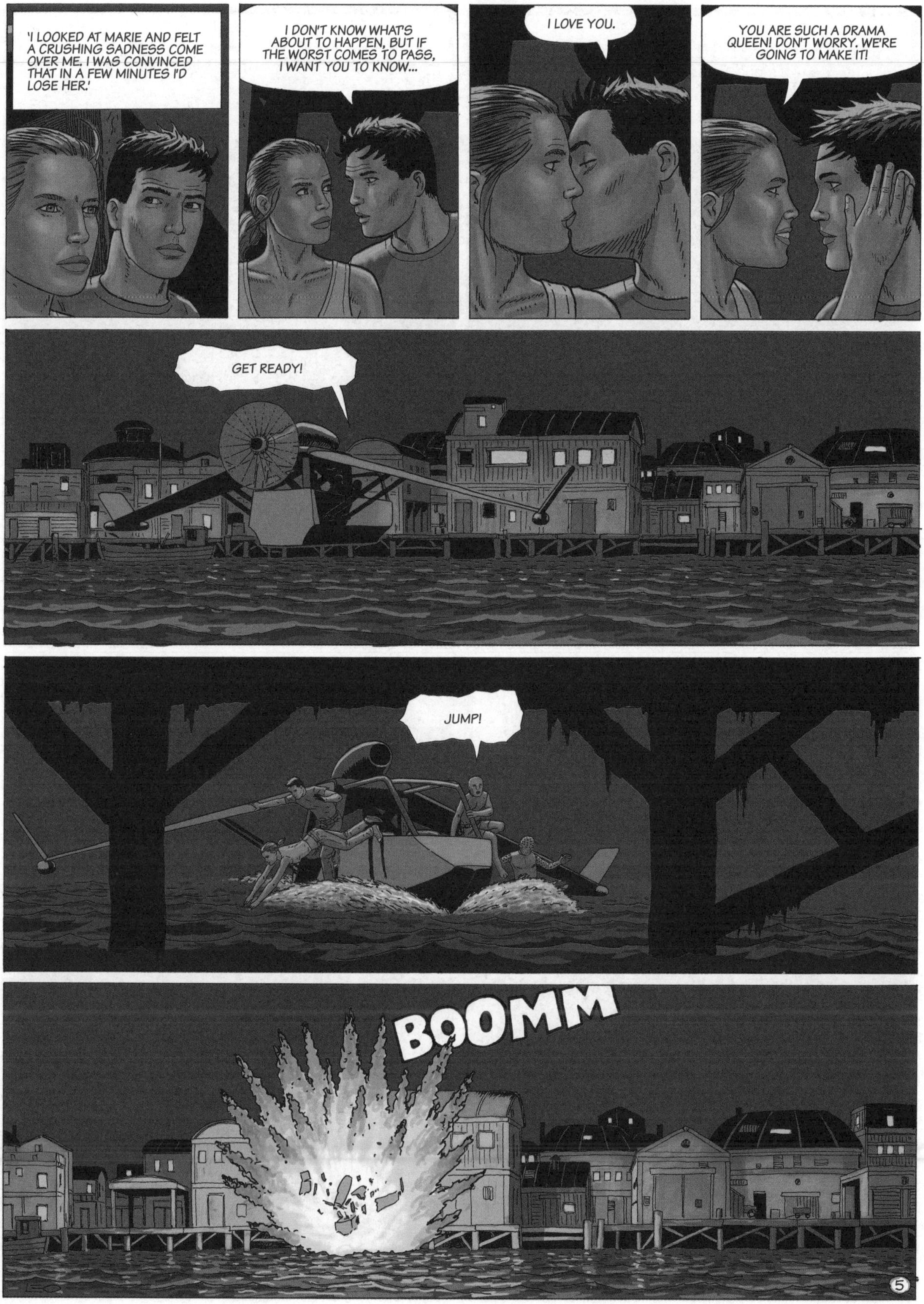
'I LOOKED AT MARIE AND FELT A CRUSHING SADNESS COME OVER ME. I WAS CONVINCED THAT IN A FEW MINUTES I'D LOSE HER.'
I DON'T KNOW WHAT'S ABOUT TO HAPPEN, BUT IF THE WORST COMES TO PASS, I WANT YOU TO KNOW...
I LOVE YOU.
YOU ARE SUCH A DRAMA QUEEN! DON'T WORRY. WE'RE GOING TO MAKE IT!
GET READY!
JUMP!
BOOMM
5

'OUR PREPOSTEROUS ASSAULT ON THE SQUIDS' RAFT-CITY WILL REMAIN SEARED IN MY MEMORY FOR EVER. WHEN, LIKE ME, YOU AREN'T USED TO VIOLENCE, WHEN IT SUDDENLY RAGES ALL AROUND YOU AND — EVEN WORSE — WHEN YOU'RE FORCED TO USE IT YOURSELF TO STAY ALIVE, IT'S A TERRIBLE SHOCK! AND THE SCARS IT LEAVES ARE DEEP, AND NEVER GO AWAY.'

'AT THE BEGINNING OF OUR ATTACK, THE SWIFTNESS AND FEROCITY OF OUR HOLORAN FRIENDS TOOK ME BY SURPRISE. THEY SWEPT THROUGH THE ALLEYS OF THAT STRANGE TOWN WITH SUCH MIND-BLOWING SPEED THAT MARIE AND I HAD A HARD TIME JUST KEEPING UP WITH THEM ... THE UPSHOT BEING THAT WE BARELY HAD A CHANCE TO LEND A HAND IN THE FIRST SKIRMISHES — MUCH TO MY RELIEF, I'LL ADMIT...'

'WE HAD TO FIND OUT QUICKLY WHERE DJAMILA WAS BEING KEPT, OF COURSE. BUT I WAS DEEPLY TROUBLED AT THE COLD, BLOODY VIOLENCE DISPLAYED BY ANTAC AND — ESPECIALLY — SELKERT. IT WAS SUCH A STARK CONTRAST TO THE CUSTOMARY KINDNESS OF THE HOLORANS...'

'EVENTUALLY THE INEVITABLE HAPPENED: ANTAC AND SELKERT CHARGED AHEAD SO FAST THAT WE LOST SIGHT OF THEM.'

LET'S GO THIS WAY!

8

'AND THE MIRACLE OCCURRED!...'

IT'S A PRISON!

'JUST LIKE THAT, ALMOST BY PURE CHANCE, WE'D FOUND DJAMILA!'

DJAMILA!

YOU CAME FOR ME! I'D ALREADY GIVEN UP!

'SOME OF THE PRISONERS THAT HAD BEEN WITH DJAMILA TOOK OUR PISTOLS, GESTURING THAT THEY INTENDED TO OPEN THE OTHER CELLS. WE DIDN'T RESIST THEM.'

'WE CHOSE TO GET OUT RIGHT AWAY AND LEAVE THEM OUR WEAPONS — AS THE BATTERIES WERE ALMOST EMPTY ANYWAY.'

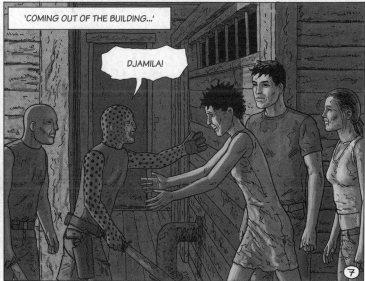

'COMING OUT OF THE BUILDING...'

DJAMILA!

'THEN WE HAD TO FIND A WAY TO ESCAPE. IT WASN'T EASY!...'

'FOR THE FIRST TIME IN MY LIFE I HAD TO WIELD A BLADE IN ANGER, HAND-TO-TENTACLE. I, WHO HAD ALWAYS LOATHED VIOLENCE!'

'AT ONE POINT, THE INCREDIBLY AGILE HOLORANS CLIMBED TO THE UPPER LEVELS, HAULING DJAMILA AFTER THEM, AND RAN...'

'...LEAVING US TO FEND FOR OURSELVES. SELKERT HAD WARNED US: THEY WOULDN'T HELP US.'

ARE YOU INJURED?!

IT'S NOTHING, JUST A SCRATCH... I THINK...

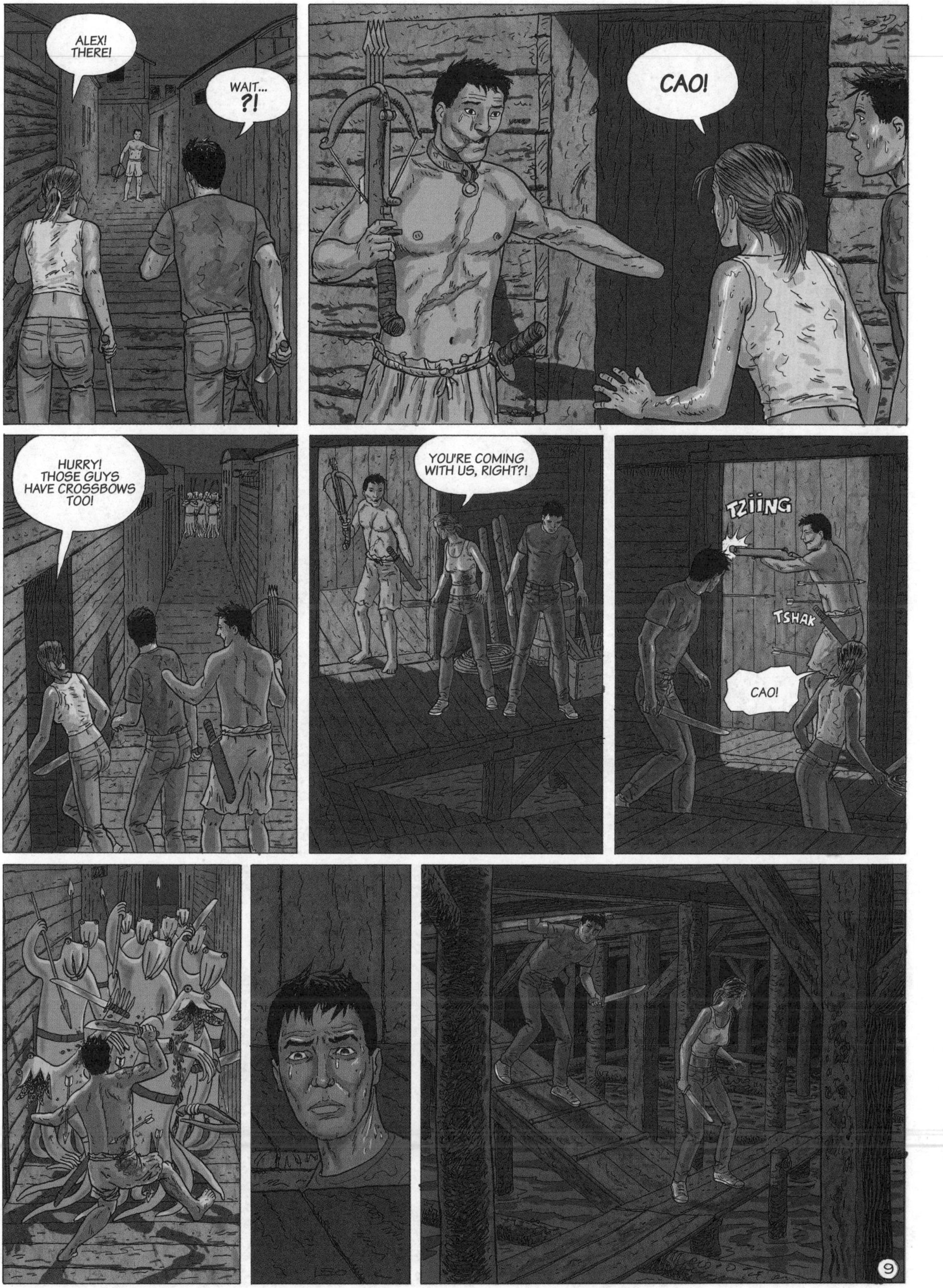

ALEX! THERE!
WAIT... ?!
CAO!
HURRY! THOSE GUYS HAVE CROSSBOWS TOO!
YOU'RE COMING WITH US, RIGHT?!
TZIING
TSHAK
CAO!
9

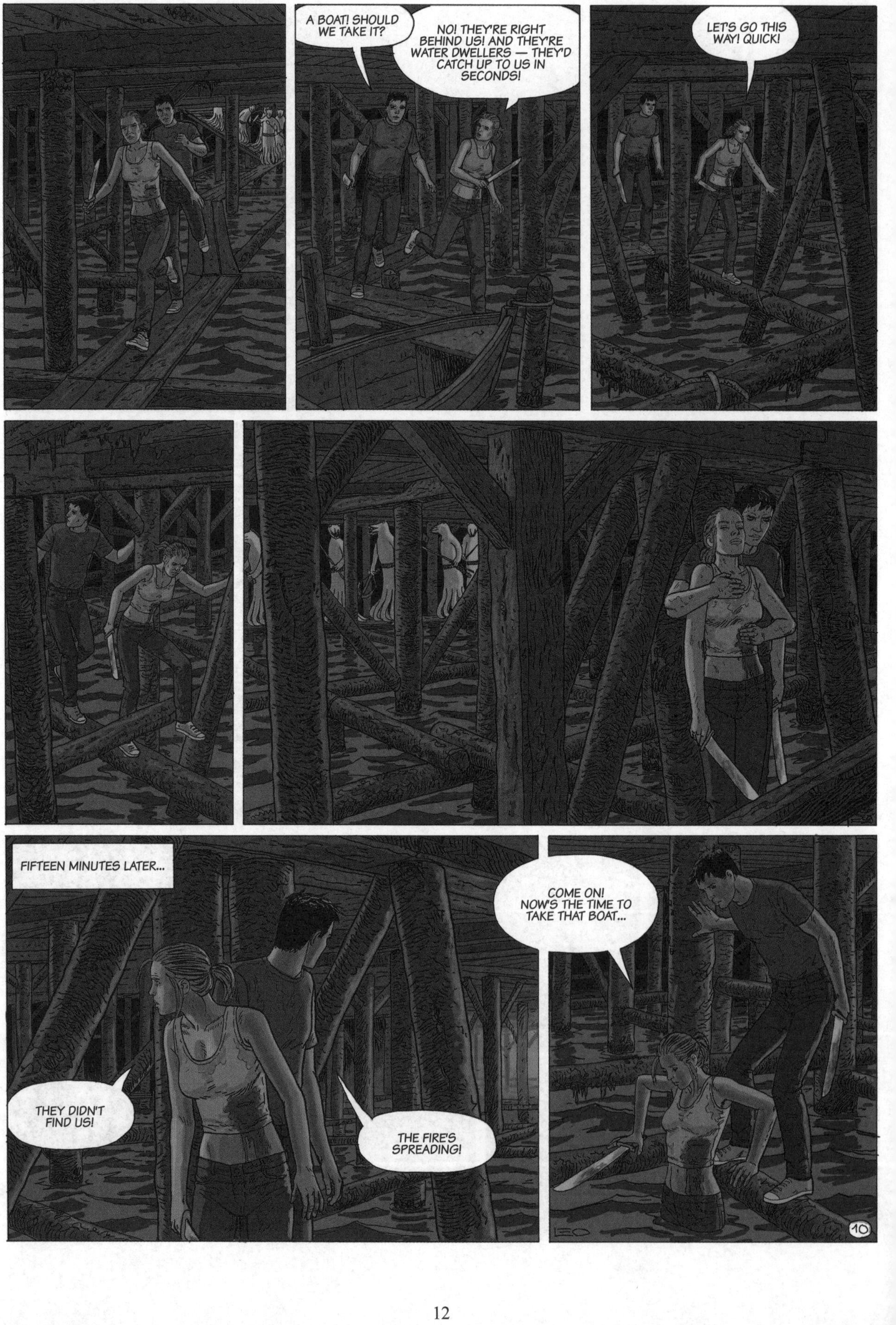
A BOAT! SHOULD WE TAKE IT?
NO! THEY'RE RIGHT BEHIND US! AND THEY'RE WATER DWELLERS — THEY'D CATCH UP TO US IN SECONDS!
LET'S GO THIS WAY! QUICK!
FIFTEEN MINUTES LATER...
THEY DIDN'T FIND US!
THE FIRE'S SPREADING!
COME ON! NOW'S THE TIME TO TAKE THAT BOAT...
LEO
10

'WE DRIFTED FOR A LONG, NERVE-RACKING TIME...'

'WE ONLY DARED CLIMB INTO THE BOAT ONCE THE FLOATING VILLAGE HAD ALMOST DISAPPEARED BELOW THE HORIZON.'

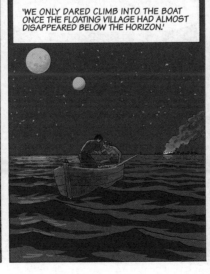

'AND A LITTLE LATER, WE RAISED THE SMALL SAIL.'

'ALL THAT WAS LEFT WAS TO MAKE IT BACK TO OUR ISLAND, WHICH WAS THE RENDEZVOUS POINT WE'D CHOSEN WITH ANTAC AND SELKERT.'

HOW'S YOUR WOUND?

STILL BLEEDING A BIT...

WE NEED TO BANDAGE IT TO CLOSE THE CUT.

DOES IT HURT?

A LITTLE, YES...

THERE! FORTUNATELY, I CAN SEE WELL ENOUGH BY THE LIGHT OF TWO MOONS!

CAO... THEY HACKED HIM TO PIECES!

WHAT THEY'VE DONE TO HIM... THE STATE OF HIM... SUCH A SHOCK! POOR CAO... I FEEL LIKE CRYING!

HE HAD NO LUCK AT ALL, DID HE?... UNLIKE US! I'M AMAZED WE SUCCEEDED! WE GOT OUT OF THIS ABSURD RAID ALIVE! IT'S INCREDIBLE!

I EVEN FOUGHT A BUNCH OF SQUIDS WITH A MACHETE... I'M JUST A STUDENT WITH NO COMBAT TRAINING AT ALL! I CAN'T BELIEVE IT!

THOSE SQUIDS LOOK POWERFUL, BUT OUT OF THE WATER THEY'RE ACTUALLY RATHER CLUMSY. AND THEIR BODIES ARE HIGHLY VULNERABLE, BECAUSE THEY DON'T HAVE A SKELETON.

12

DO YOU THINK ANTAC AND SELKERT MADE IT OUT TOO? WITH DJAMILA?

I THINK SO, YES. THOSE TWO ARE RESOURCEFUL AND SKILLED!

AND DON'T FORGET SUPER VIOLENT! DID YOU SEE THEM? ESPECIALLY SELKERT! IT WAS KIND OF SCARY.

YES, I WAS SURPRISED BY HOW CLINICALLY THEY KILLED, TOO.

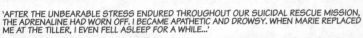

'AFTER THE UNBEARABLE STRESS ENDURED THROUGHOUT OUR SUICIDAL RESCUE MISSION, THE ADRENALINE HAD WORN OFF. I BECAME APATHETIC AND DROWSY. WHEN MARIE REPLACED ME AT THE TILLER, I EVEN FELL ASLEEP FOR A WHILE...'

ALEX!

HMM?...

THE ISLAND! YOU MANAGED TO FIND IT! WELL DONE, MARIE!

HOW ARE YOU FEELING? YOUR WOUND?

IT'S NO LONGER BLEEDING — THAT'S SOMETHING!...

THANK GOODNESS THE BLADE DIDN'T HIT YOUR BREAST. I'D HAVE BEEN DEVASTATED IF SUCH A MAGNIFICENT BUST HAD BEEN DAMAGED.

AND SO WOULD I!

NO ONE IN SIGHT! I WAS HOPING WE'D FIND THEM HERE.

MAYBE THEY HAD A HARDER TIME FINDING A BOAT OR SNEAKING AWAY.

13

NO! WE NEED TO SINK THE BOAT, LIKE WE DID WITH OURS. WE MUSTN'T BETRAY OUR PRESENCE HERE!

OH, THERE YOU ARE! I'M SO RELIEVED!

SO ARE WE. WE WERE ALMOST CERTAIN YOU WOULDN'T MAKE IT OUT!

DJAMILA! I'M SO HAPPY TO SEE YOU AGAIN!

HAVE YOU HEARD ABOUT THE EXTENT OF THE TIME JUMP?

I STILL HAVEN'T WRAPPED MY HEAD AROUND IT!...

TO THINK I'LL NEVER SEE THEM AGAIN!... MY BROTHER, PAM, ILSE, MAX... ON THE ONE HAND, I'M OVERJOYED AT BEING FREE FROM THAT NIGHTMARISH PRISON. ON THE OTHER, THERE'S THIS OVERWHELMING SADNESS. I FEEL TORN IN TWO... I CAN'T EVEN CRY.

IT WAS EASY — THERE'S A TRAPDOOR AT THE BOTTOM.

BUT A BOAT COULD BE QUITE HANDY, COULDN'T IT?

WE CAN ALWAYS REFLOAT IT IF WE NEED IT. RIGHT NOW THE IMPORTANT PART IS TO BE STEALTHY. THE SQUIDS WILL PROBABLY COME LOOKING FOR US — WE HUMILIATED THEM!

YOU'RE INJURED. LET ME TAKE A LOOK.

JUST A FLESH WOUND, BUT WE CAN'T LET IT BECOME INFECTED.

THERE. LET'S BANDAGE IT AGAIN.

COME ON! WE NEED TO GET OFF THE BEACH AND ERASE OUR TRACKS. THE SQUIDS COULD SHOW UP AT ANY TIME — THEY'RE EXTREMELY FAST SWIMMERS!

HOW LONG WERE YOU A PRISONER, DJAMILA? IT WAS ONLY A DAY FOR US, BUT WITH THE TEMPORAL LEAP...?

OH, IF ONLY IT HAD BEEN JUST A DAY!... IN FACT, I WAS THERE FOR AT LEAST THREE MONTHS! I'M AFRAID I LOST COUNT.

THREE MONTHS! YOU POOR THING ...

AND DON'T ASK ME ABOUT THAT TIME. I HAVE ABSOLUTELY NO DESIRE TO TALK ABOUT IT!

WE CAME ACROSS CAO ...

YES, HE WAS THERE WHEN I ARRIVED. ANOTHER CRAZY COINCIDENCE!... I PROBABLY WOULDN'T HAVE SURVIVED WITHOUT HIS HELP...

HE SAVED OUR LIVES TOO...

AND IT COST HIM HIS!

POOR CAO! WE COULD BARELY COMMUNICATE. HE COULDN'T SPEAK ANY MORE BECAUSE OF HIS FACIAL INJURIES. I NEVER FOUND OUT WHAT HAPPENED TO HIM. MAYBE HE'S BETTER OFF NOW — HE WAS IN CONSTANT, TERRIBLE PAIN!

WHY DO THOSE SQUIDS TAKE CAPTIVES LIKE THAT? WE SAW DOZENS OF THEM, OF MANY RACES.

GOOD QUESTION. I GUESS WHEN SO MANY DIFFERENT SPECIES MUST LIVE TOGETHER, VIOLENCE IS NEVER FAR AWAY...

FRESH WATER. WE WON'T DIE OF THIRST...

15

I SAY WE SET UP CAMP HERE.

WHAT'S THE PLAN? WHAT ARE WE GOING TO DO?

SHORT TERM, THE MAIN THING IS TO PROTECT OURSELVES FROM THE SQUID THREAT. WHICH MEANS STAY OUT OF SIGHT, BECAUSE THE BATTERIES IN OUR WEAPONS ARE DEAD.

FOR A FEW DAYS WE WON'T BE BUILDING ANY SHELTER OR LIGHTING ANY FIRES. WE'LL EAT FRUITS AND ROOTS.

'IN OTHER WORDS, WE COULD LOOK FORWARD TO A LONG STRETCH OF DIFFICULTY AND UNPLEASANTNESS! EXTREME LACK OF COMFORT AND SURVIVAL-LEVEL NUTRITION.'

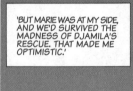

'BUT MARIE WAS AT MY SIDE, AND WE'D SURVIVED THE MADNESS OF DJAMILA'S RESCUE. THAT MADE ME OPTIMISTIC.'

I DON'T KNOW ABOUT YOU, BUT I'M ABSOLUTELY STARVING!

YES, SO AM I.

'THE FIRST FEW DAYS WERE VERY ROUGH. THERE WASN'T A LOT OF EDIBLE FRUIT ON THE ISLAND.'

'ON THE FOURTH DAY, JUST AS WE WERE ABOUT TO RISK GOING DOWN TO THE BEACH TO FISH, WE SAW A GROUP OF SQUIDS MAKE LAND. IT WAS OBVIOUS THEY WERE LOOKING FOR US.'

16

'FORTUNATELY, THEY REMAINED ON THE BEACH AND LEFT AFTER HALF AN HOUR. WE DEDUCED THAT THEIR SEMI-AQUATIC ANATOMY MADE PROGRESS THROUGH THE ISLAND'S DENSE VEGETATION DIFFICULT.'

'TWO DAYS AFTER THE SQUIDS' DEPARTURE, WE CAME DOWN FROM THE HEIGHTS TO FISH, AND OUR DIET IMPROVED CONSIDERABLY.'

'THEN DJAMILA GOT SICK. SHE HAD STOMACH PAINS AND A HIGH FEVER. PROBABLY A RESULT OF THE MISTREATMENT SHE'D RECEIVED FROM THE SQUIDS WHILE IN THEIR PRISON.'

'SELKERT TRIED TO TREAT HER WITH INFUSIONS. SHE'D SCOUR THE ISLAND TO FIND THE RIGHT PLANTS. BUT TO NO AVAIL. DJAMILA'S CONDITION KEPT GETTING WORSE.'

'FORTUNATELY, AT LEAST MARIE'S WOUND WAS INFECTION-FREE AND HEALING.'

'THEN, ONE MORNING...'

A SHIP!

THAT'S OUR PEOPLE!

YOU'RE RIGHT!

WHAT?!

BUT HOW DO YOU KNOW ?!

THAT FLAG! IT'S THE SYMBOL OF OUR SPACE UNIT!

'IMMEDIATELY WE LIT A BIG FIRE TO LET THEM KNOW WE WERE THERE.'

IT'S SUCH A RELIEF, ALEX!

THERE'S SOMETHING I DON'T UNDERSTAND ...

IF 93 YEARS HAVE GONE BY, WHY DID THEY DECIDE TO COME LOOKING FOR US AFTER SO LONG? IT DOESN'T MAKE SENSE! UNLESS...

WHAT, ANTAC?...

'THAT WAS WHEN I SAW THEM!...'

18

BUT HOW IS THAT POSSIBLE?! THAT WOULD MEAN THAT THEY ALSO...

YES, THEY MADE A GIANT TEMPORAL LEAP TOO, LIKE OURS. THAT EXPLAINS WHY THEY'RE HERE! TALK ABOUT A STROKE OF LUCK!

THIS IS ABSOLUTELY UNBELIEVABLE! YOU'RE ALIVE! YOU'VE GONE THROUGH A TIME JUMP JUST LIKE US!

WHAT ABOUT DJAMILA AND SELKERT? WHERE ARE THEY?

DJAMILA IS SLIGHTLY ILL. SELKERT STAYED WITH HER. WE'LL GO GET THEM.

I'LL GO WITH YOU!

MARIE! I'M SO GLAD TO SEE YOU AGAIN!

MAX!

MY GOD, ILSE! YOU'RE HERE! YOU'RE ALIVE!...

'AS I HELD ILSE TIGHT, I FELT THE SLIGHTEST HESITATION FROM HER. SO I ASKED THE OBVIOUS QUESTION...'

HOW LONG AGO DID YOU GO THROUGH THE TIME DISTORTION? IT'S ONLY BEEN A FEW DAYS HERE...

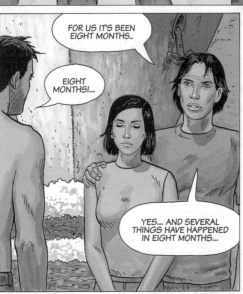

FOR US IT'S BEEN EIGHT MONTHS..

EIGHT MONTHS!...

YES... AND SEVERAL THINGS HAVE HAPPENED IN EIGHT MONTHS...

FOR ONE THING, ILSE AND I ARE TOGETHER NOW. WE THOUGHT YOU WERE LONG DEAD...

YOU UNDERSTAND, DON'T YOU, ALEX? WHEN WE FOUND OUT WE'D JUMPED 93 YEARS AHEAD, WE HAD TO COME TO TERMS WITH THE IDEA THAT WE'D NEVER SEE YOU OR MARIE AGAIN...

OF COURSE I UNDERSTAND, ILSE. WE THOUGHT THE SAME THING...

SO? WHAT'S WRONG WITH HER?

IT LOOKS LIKE A KIDNEY INFECTION, AND SHE'S UNDER-NOURISHED. BUT IT'S NOTHING SERIOUS. SHE'LL SOON BE BACK ON HER FEET.

WHAT'S THE PLAN? ARE WE GOING TO STAY HERE A WHILE? OR ARE WE GOING HOME?

I DON'T KNOW YET. IN THE MEANTIME, THOUGH, I'M GOING TO FIND YOU A CABIN.

20

I'M GUESSING THAT ONE CABIN WILL WORK FOR THE TWO OF YOU... OR AM I COMPLETELY WRONG?

NO, YOU'RE NOT WRONG...

OF COURSE I'M NOT! WHAT CHANCE DID THAT POOR ALEX HAVE OF ESCAPING YOUR IRRESISTIBLE CHARM, MARIE?

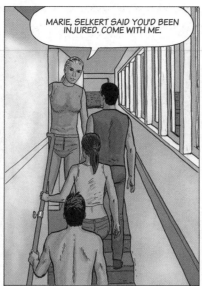

MARIE, SELKERT SAID YOU'D BEEN INJURED. COME WITH ME.

HERE. IT'S SMALL, BUT COZY.

IT'S HEAVEN, HAKIM! WE'VE BEEN SLEEPING ON THE GROUND FOR DAYS!

THERE'S A SHOWER AT THE END OF THE HALLWAY.

YOU KNOW WHAT? FATE HAS FINALLY STRAIGHTENED THINGS OUT. I'VE ALWAYS THOUGHT THAT YOU AND MARIE WERE MADE FOR EACH OTHER.

YOU'RE 100 PERCENT RIGHT, HAKIM!

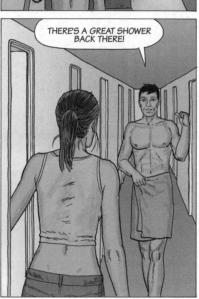

THERE'S A GREAT SHOWER BACK THERE!

THIS BANDAGE IS FANTASTIC! IT ISOLATES THE WOUND COMPLETELY, AND IT INCLUDES A TOPICAL ANAESTHETIC. I DON'T FEEL A THING ANY MORE!

OH... I'M SORRY.

ILSE, COME IN!

I JUST CAME TO BRING YOU YOUR CLOTHES... WE'D KEPT THEM, OF COURSE...

ILSE!

YES?

WHEN YOU AND ALEX WERE TOGETHER BEFORE... THERE WAS NOTHING BETWEEN US BACK THEN.

ALL RIGHT... I BELIEVE YOU.

21

23

ARE YOU SURE ABOUT WHAT YOU JUST SAID?

HMM... MAYBE NOT ...

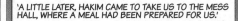

'A LITTLE LATER, HAKIM CAME TO TAKE US TO THE MESS HALL, WHERE A MEAL HAD BEEN PREPARED FOR US.'

ANTAC AND SELKERT REPORTED ON THE STRANGE PHENOMENA YOU WITNESSED HERE, AND THE DECISION'S BEEN MADE TO STAY IN THE AREA FOR A WHILE.

BUT TONIGHT WE'LL BE HEADING TO ANOTHER ISLAND NOT TOO FAR AWAY. A MUCH BIGGER ISLAND, BECAUSE WE NEED TO REFILL OUR FRESH WATER TANKS AND RESTOCK ON FRESH FRUIT.

'OUR FIRST MEAL ABOARD THE SHIP. THE MOOD WAS HAPPY, OF COURSE. ANOTHER ONE OF THOSE SUDDEN REVERSALS OF SITUATION. JUST A FEW HOURS BEFORE, WE'D BEEN IN DIRE STRAITS — ALMOST DESPERATE!'

'AND A FEW DAYS EARLIER, I'D BEEN WITH ILSE, IN WHAT I THOUGHT WOULD BE A LASTING RELATIONSHIP. NOW, I WAS WITH MARIE. IT WASN'T EASY DEALING WITH ALL THAT!'

'HAKIM EXPLAINED THE HOLORANS' THEORY ON WHAT HAD HAPPENED: THE QUANTUM ANOMALY THAT HAD HIT US, CAUSING OUR HUGE TIME JUMP, HAD COVERED A MASSIVE AREA ALL AT ONCE. IT HAD ALSO BEEN STAR-SHAPED.'

AND APPARENTLY, THERE WERE SMALL TEMPORAL DIFFERENCES BETWEEN ALL THE BRANCHES OF THAT STAR.

THIS IS INSANE! JUMPING FORWARD A HUNDRED YEARS INTO THE FUTURE! OUR PARENTS, OUR FRIENDS BACK ON EARTH... THEY'RE ALL LONG DEAD!

YES. COMING TO TERMS WITH THAT WAS PRETTY HARD.

22

'WE STAYED THERE, CHATTING, AFTER EATING. OUR FRIENDS MOSTLY WANTED MARIE AND ME TO TELL THEM WHAT HAD HAPPENED TO US DURING OUR TRIP.'

'EVENTUALLY WE BEGAN LAPSING INTO SILENCE MORE AND MORE, AND MARIE CHOSE ONE OF THOSE MOMENTS TO LEAN TOWARDS ME AND WHISPER IN MY EAR...'

WHY DON'T WE GET OUT OF HERE? I WANT YOU.

'OH, MARIE, MARIE, YOU ARE THE MOST ADORABLE WOMAN IN THE WORLD! WE EXCUSED OURSELVES, CLAIMING A RATHER UNDERSTANDABLE EXHAUSTION, AND LEFT.'

THERE! WE'RE FINALLY GOING TO BE ABLE TO MAKE LOVE IN A COMFORTABLE BED, WITHOUT SCRAPING OUR SKIN ON ROCKS LIKE THE FIRST TIME!...

I'M RELIEVED, YOU KNOW. I WASN'T ENTIRELY SURE YOU'D BE INTERESTED...

AND WHY IS THAT?

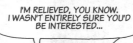

BECAUSE YOU'RE A BIT OF A COMPLICATED GIRL, MARIE SERVOZ, AND SOMETIMES I HAVE A HARD TIME FIGURING OUT WHAT YOU REALLY WANT.

THEN STOP TALKING AND GET INTO BED! BEFORE I CHANGE MY MIND...

'WHAT A MAGICAL NIGHT WE HAD, CUT OFF FROM THE WORLD IN OUR COZY LITTLE CABIN!...'

'FOR THE FIRST TIME, MARIE LOWERED HER DEFENCES AND LET ME IN WITHOUT HOLDING BACK. FROM THAT NIGHT ON, I WAS CERTAIN THAT THE TWO OF US WERE TRULY TOGETHER.'

23

OH, MAN, I SLEPT SO WELL!

WERE YOU ALREADY AWAKE? AND WATCHING ME?

YES... YOU'RE VERY BEAUTIFUL WHEN YOU SLEEP.

WE'RE ALMOST THERE! THE ISLAND ISN'T FAR NOW!

24

HERE. EVERYONE TAKE A BASKET AND START PICKING THOSE APPLE-LIKE FRUIT THAT GROW ON SAND. THEY'RE DELICIOUS.

CHOOSE THE ONES THAT AREN'T TOO RIPE. THEY'LL KEEP BETTER. AND THE BEST ONES ARE THE PURPLE ONES — BUT THEY'RE RARER.

IF YOU'RE HEADING THAT WAY, ALEX AND I WILL GO IN THE OTHER DIRECTION.

ALL RIGHT — BUT DON'T GO TOO FAR.

DO YOU KNOW WHY I DIDN'T OFFER TO GO WITH THEM?

ER... NO.

BECAUSE MAX AND ILSE ARE VERY UNCOMFORTABLE AROUND US. HAVEN'T YOU NOTICED?

NOT REALLY, NO.... I SUPPOSE IT'S UNDERSTANDABLE, ISN'T IT?

25

'IF MARIE OR I HAD TURNED ROUND AS WE WERE CLIMBING OVER THE ROCKS, OUR FATES WOULD CERTAINLY HAVE BEEN COMPLETELY DIFFERENT.'

'WE WOULD HAVE SEEN THE DANGER COMING AND WOULD NO DOUBT HAVE RETURNED TO THE SHIP. BUT WE DIDN'T.'

LOOK! A WHOLE BUNCH OF PURPLE APPLES!

OUR BASKETS WILL BE PURPLE ALL THE WAY!

AH!

THIS THING IS UGLY AS SIN!

FRY IT, MARIE! NO POINT IN TAKING CHANCES.

CLICK CLICK

IT'S NOT WORKING!

WHAT?!

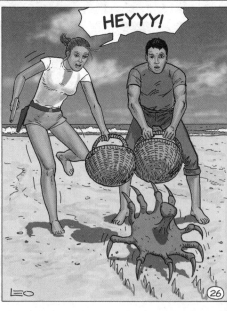

HEYYY!

LEO

26

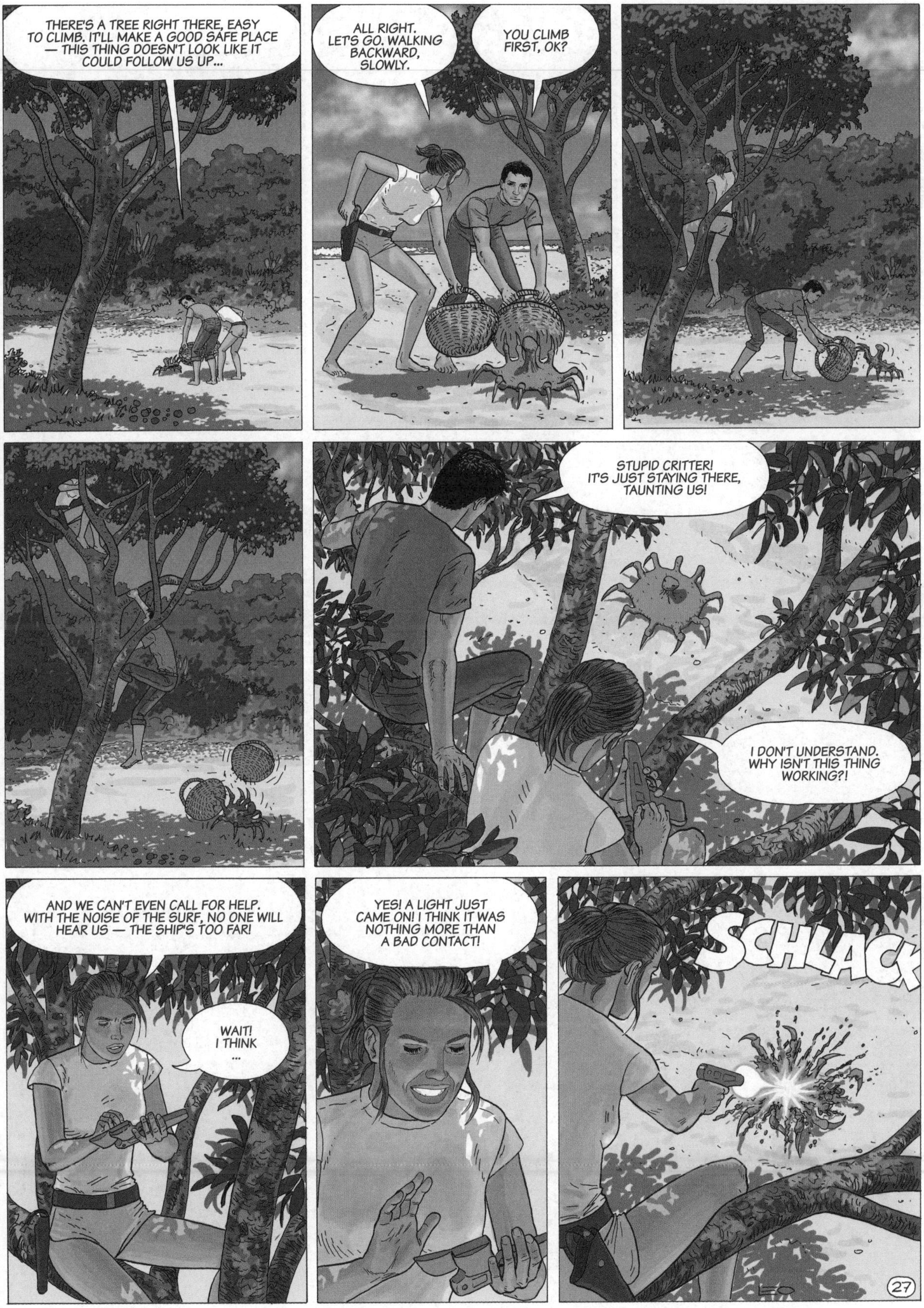
THERE'S A TREE RIGHT THERE, EASY TO CLIMB. IT'LL MAKE A GOOD SAFE PLACE — THIS THING DOESN'T LOOK LIKE IT COULD FOLLOW US UP...
ALL RIGHT. LET'S GO. WALKING BACKWARD, SLOWLY.
YOU CLIMB FIRST, OK?
STUPID CRITTER! IT'S JUST STAYING THERE, TAUNTING US!
I DON'T UNDERSTAND. WHY ISN'T THIS THING WORKING?!
AND WE CAN'T EVEN CALL FOR HELP. WITH THE NOISE OF THE SURF, NO ONE WILL HEAR US — THE SHIP'S TOO FAR!
WAIT! I THINK ...
YES! A LIGHT JUST CAME ON! I THINK IT WAS NOTHING MORE THAN A BAD CONTACT!
SCHLACK
LEO
27

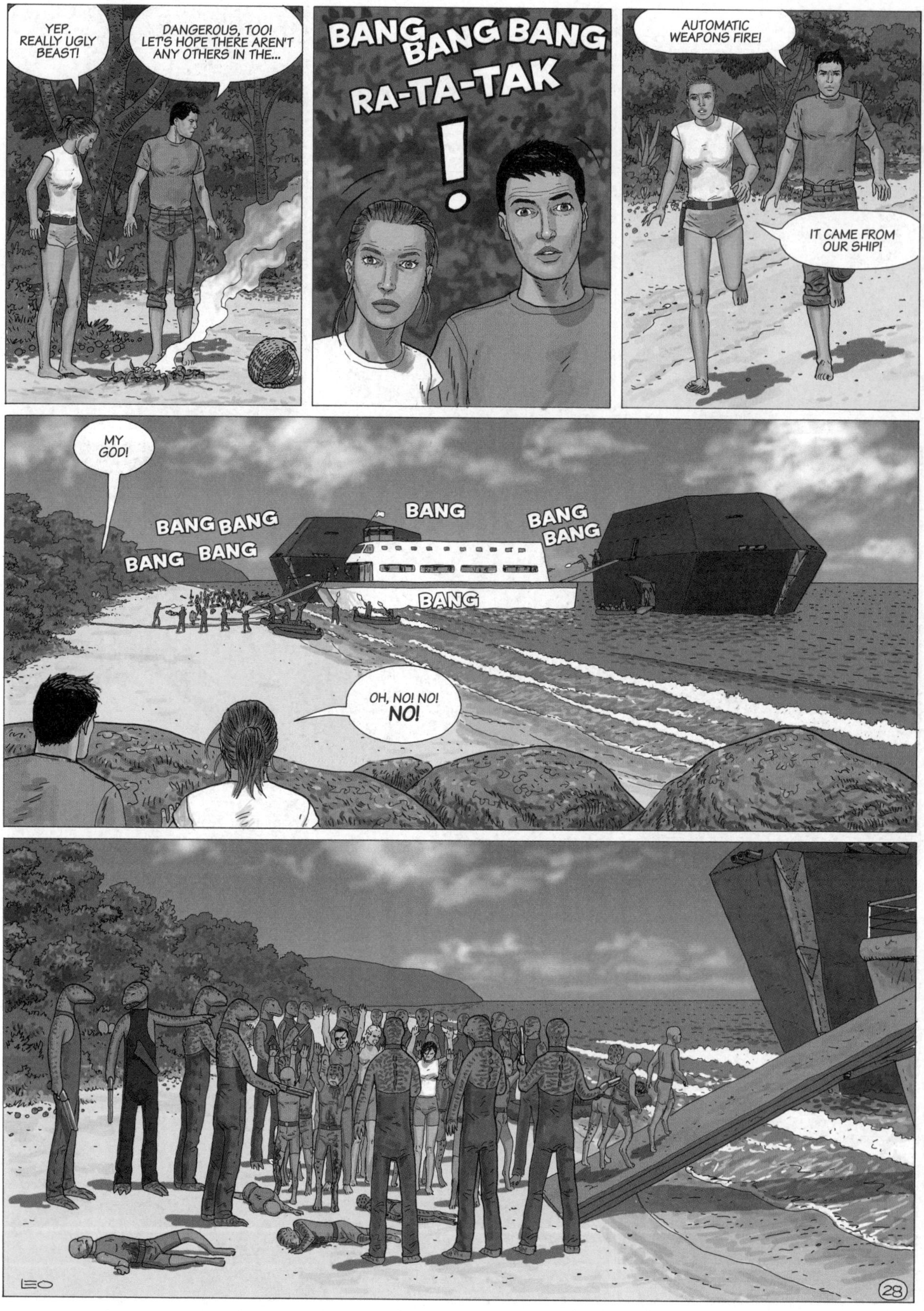

YEP. REALLY UGLY BEAST!
DANGEROUS, TOO! LET'S HOPE THERE AREN'T ANY OTHERS IN THE...
BANG BANG BANG
RA-TA-TAK
!
AUTOMATIC WEAPONS FIRE!
IT CAME FROM OUR SHIP!
MY GOD!
BANG BANG
BANG BANG
BANG
BANG BANG
BANG
OH, NO! NO! NO!
LEO
28

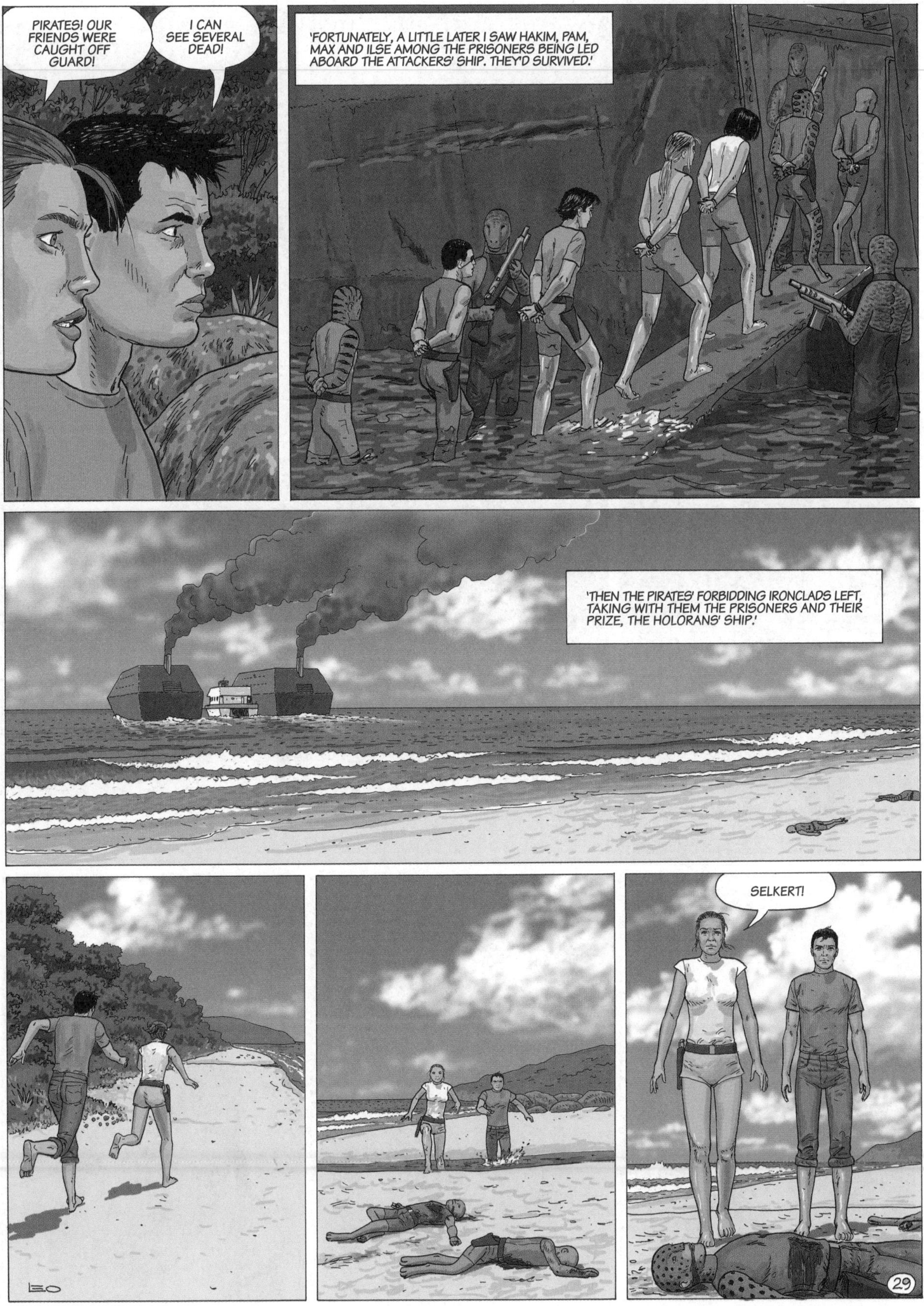
PIRATES! OUR FRIENDS WERE CAUGHT OFF GUARD!
I CAN SEE SEVERAL DEAD!
'FORTUNATELY, A LITTLE LATER I SAW HAKIM, PAM, MAX AND ILSE AMONG THE PRISONERS BEING LED ABOARD THE ATTACKERS' SHIP. THEY'D SURVIVED.'
'THEN THE PIRATES' FORBIDDING IRONCLADS LEFT, TAKING WITH THEM THE PRISONERS AND THEIR PRIZE, THE HOLORANS' SHIP.'
SELKERT!
LEO
29

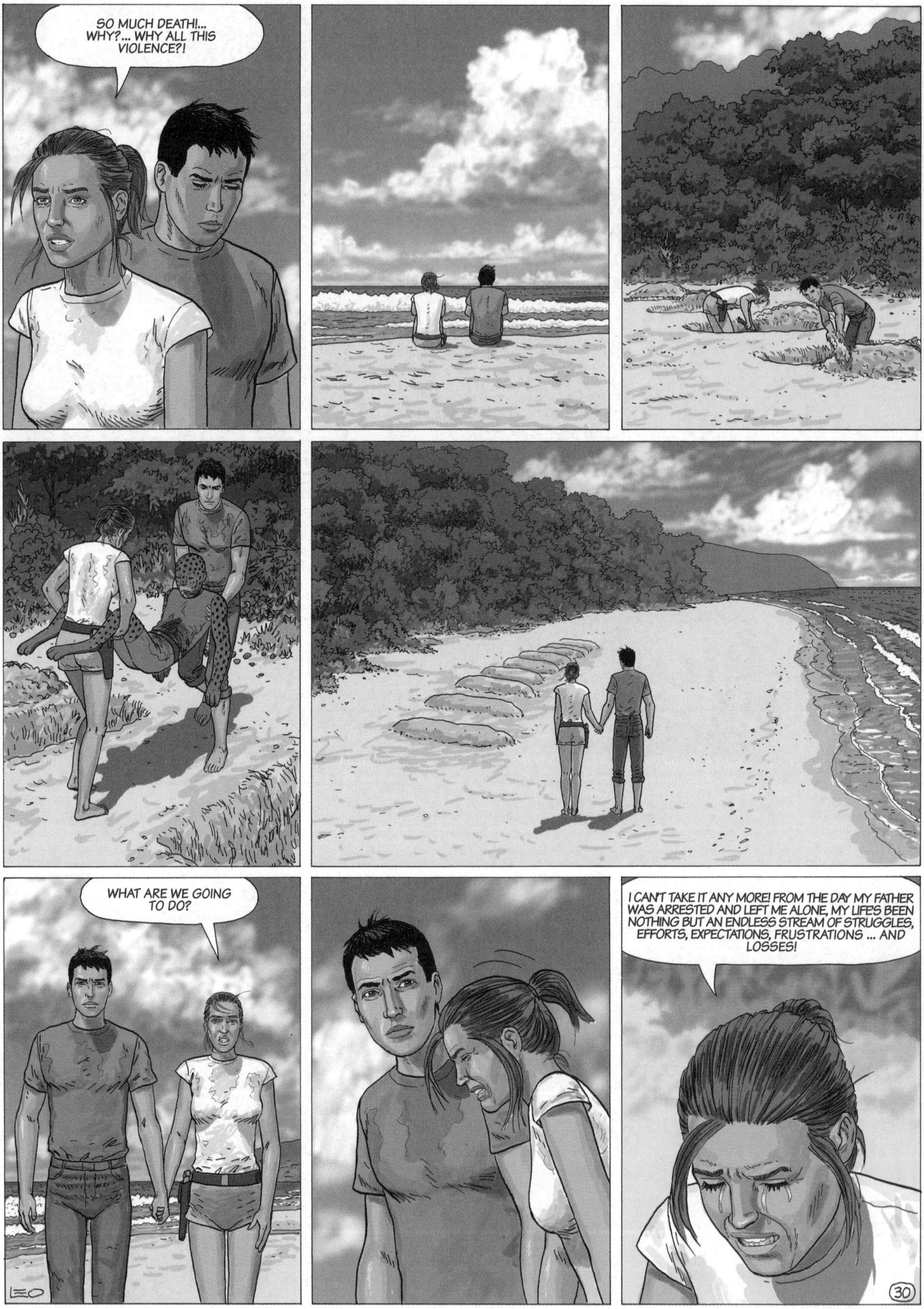
SO MUCH DEATH!... WHY?... WHY ALL THIS VIOLENCE?!
WHAT ARE WE GOING TO DO?
I CAN'T TAKE IT ANY MORE! FROM THE DAY MY FATHER WAS ARRESTED AND LEFT ME ALONE, MY LIFE'S BEEN NOTHING BUT AN ENDLESS STREAM OF STRUGGLES, EFFORTS, EXPECTATIONS, FRUSTRATIONS ... AND LOSSES!
LEO
30

AND EVER SINCE WE ARRIVED ON THIS DAMNED PLANET, EVERYTHING'S BEEN UNCERTAINTY AND MORTAL DANGER!

AFTER THE CONSTANT TENSION DEALING WITH THOSE HORRIBLE SQUIDS, WE WERE FINALLY NICE AND SAFE ON THE HOLORANS' WONDERFUL SHIP, AND NOW... THE NIGHTMARE'S RETURNED!

WE'RE BACK ON SQUARE ONE! NO IDEA WHERE TO GO! NO IDEA WHAT TO DO! NO IDEA WHETHER WE'LL STILL BE ALIVE TOMORROW!

SORRY. I LOST IT FOR A MOMENT...

YOU HAVE NOTHING TO APOLOGISE FOR.

'OOF! SEEING A WOMAN AS TOUGH AS MARIE SOBBING WITH DESPAIR... THAT'S HORRIBLY UNSETTLING! I HAD TO MAKE AN ENORMOUS EFFORT TO KEEP FROM CRACKING TOO.'

LET'S GET AWAY FROM HERE. I DON'T WANT TO SEE THESE GRAVES ANY MORE!

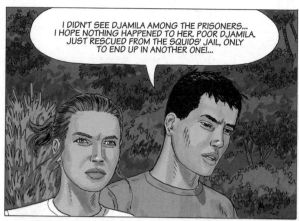

I DIDN'T SEE DJAMILA AMONG THE PRISONERS... I HOPE NOTHING HAPPENED TO HER. POOR DJAMILA. JUST RESCUED FROM THE SQUIDS' JAIL, ONLY TO END UP IN ANOTHER ONE!...

CAN WE NOT TALK ABOUT THIS FOR A WHILE? IT'S LIKE RUBBING SALT INTO THE WOUND!

YOU'RE RIGHT, OF COURSE. I'M SORRY.

'AFTER WALKING FOR AN HOUR OR SO, HUNGER AND THIRST FORCED US TO STOP. FORTUNATELY, THERE WERE JUICY SAND APPLES EVERYWHERE!'

I SAW ON THAT MAP ON THE SHIP THAT THIS ISLAND'S NOT FAR FROM A MUCH LARGER LAND MASS SOMEWHERE IN THAT DIRECTION. THAT'S OUR GOAL NOW: FIND A WAY TO SAIL ACROSS TO IT.

WE'LL NEVER SURVIVE HERE FOR LONG.

ARE YOU SURE IT'S THAT WAY? WHAT MAP ARE YOU TALKING ABOUT?

AT THE ENTRANCE TO THE MESS HALL, ALEX. THERE WAS THAT HUGE MAP WITH A TON OF ANNOTATIONS. DIDN'T YOU NOTICE IT?

ER... NO.

YOU HAVE TO PAY MORE ATTENTION TO YOUR SURROUNDINGS, ALEX. YOU SHOULDN'T JUST RELY ON ME.

'YES, BEING WITH A WOMAN LIKE MARIE-THE-COMPUTER WASN'T ALWAYS EASY!...'

'SO WE HAD A GOAL: SAILING ACROSS. BUT THAT IMPLIED BUILDING A BOAT! A GOOD ENOUGH BOAT TO BRAVE THE OPEN SEAS! I WASN'T TOO OPTIMISTIC ABOUT OUR CHANCES OF ACCOMPLISHING SUCH A FEAT...'

'...BUT I WAS CAREFUL NOT TO SHOW MARIE MY SCEPTICISM.'

LOOK AT THE SIZE OF THAT BIRD!

UH-OH! IT COULD BE DANGEROUS! LET'S GET OFF THE BEACH. WE CAN MOVE UNDER COVER OF THE TREES.

HURRY! IT'S SPOTTED US!

FALSE ALARM! IT'S JUST LEAVING.

A VILLAGE!

AND IT LOOKS LIKE THEY WERE HIT BY THE SAME GUYS WHO ATTACKED OUR SHIP!

ANOTHER MASSACRE!

WHY SO MUCH VIOLENCE? WHY COME HERE TO STRIKE AT A SMALL GROUP OF PEOPLE STRUGGLING TO SURVIVE?!

IT DOESN'T MAKE SENSE! NOTHING MAKES SENSE ON THIS PLANET! EVERYTHING'S BIZARRE.

ALEX! THERE'S A BOAT HERE — IT LOOKS LIKE IT'S INTACT!

THIS IS A MOTORBOAT, ISN'T IT?

I THINK SO... THIS MUST BE THE THROTTLE CONTROL. LET'S PUSH IT OUT!

LET ME SEE... HOW DO YOU START THE ENGINE?...

HA! YOU JUST PUSH THE LEVER. IT'S AN ELECTRIC ENGINE.

ALEX, HOW ABOUT WE TRY CROSSING WITH THIS BOAT?

DO YOU THINK IT'LL HANDLE THE HIGH SEAS? OR HAVE THE RANGE?

IT LOOKS PRETTY STURDY...

THESE BATTERIES SEEM ADVANCED ENOUGH...

EVEN ON EARTH WE KNOW HOW TO BUILD POWER CELLS THAT LAST 200 YEARS.

OK... LET'S DO IT! ANYWAY, WE CAN'T STAY ON THIS ISLAND KNOWING THE BASTARDS WHO TOOK OUR SHIP COULD COME BACK AT ANY TIME.

WE NEED TO PREPARE FOR THE CROSSING. TO START WITH, IT'D BE A GOOD IDEA TO STOCK UP ON SAND APPLES AND FRESH WATER.

ABSOLUTELY.

LEO

MARIE! I THINK I'VE FOUND THE LARDER! IT'S FULL OF TINS AND DRIED FISH.

35

AND THERE'S DRINKING WATER TOO!

REALLY?! LUCK IS ON OUR SIDE FOR ONCE!

'WE STOPPED ON A BEACH A LITTLE FURTHER, NEXT TO A SMALL STREAM. WE FILLED UP THE POTABLE WATER TANK AND GATHERED A BUNCH OF APPLES.'

'AND THEN WE WERE OFF.'

'DESPITE THE LOSS OF OUR COMPANIONS, WE FELT EXHILARATED, THANKS TO THIS NEW TWIST IN OUR FORTUNES. DEEP DOWN, THOUGH, I KNEW THAT WE WERE STILL IN A PRECARIOUS SITUATION. WE HAD NO GUARANTEE THAT OUR BOAT COULD HANDLE THE OPEN OCEAN OR THAT ITS BATTERIES WOULD LAST THE WHOLE CROSSING.'

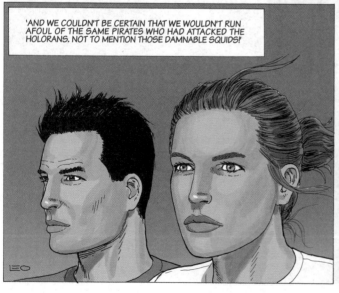

'AND WE COULDN'T BE CERTAIN THAT WE WOULDN'T RUN AFOUL OF THE SAME PIRATES WHO HAD ATTACKED THE HOLORANS. NOT TO MENTION THOSE DAMNABLE SQUIDS!'

'AT FIRST, THE TRIP WAS QUITE PEACEFUL. BY THE TIME LAND DROPPED OUT OF SIGHT BEHIND US, THOUGH, A PRONOUNCED SWELL STARTED TO TAKE ITS TOLL ON US!'

36

'A FEW HOURS LATER, FORTUNATELY, THE SEA WAS CALM AGAIN. BUT BEFORE OUR EARLIER GOOD MOOD HAD A CHANCE TO RETURN, WE HAD OUR FIRST ENCOUNTER WITH THE MARINE WILDLIFE...'

WHOA! MARIE!

RRRRR

SHLACK

DID YOU SEE THAT?! IT LOOKED LIKE AN APE! AN AQUATIC APE!

TERRIFYING! WE'RE LUCKY WE HAVE THE PISTOL!

37

LET'S JUST HOPE IT WAS ALONE AND NOT PART OF A TROOP!

'FORTUNATELY, IT WAS, AND WE WERE ABLE TO RESUME OUR JOURNEY SAFELY.'

'WHEN NIGHT CAME, WE DECIDED TO STOP TO EAT AND SLEEP. WE OPENED SOME OF THE ALIENS' TINNED FOOD.'

THIS STUFF'S GOOD!

YES, DELICIOUS!

'WHEN THE TIME CAME TO REST, THE SEA WAS STILL AND ALL SEEMED PEACEFUL. BUT UNLIKE MARIE, I COULDN'T FIND SLEEP...'

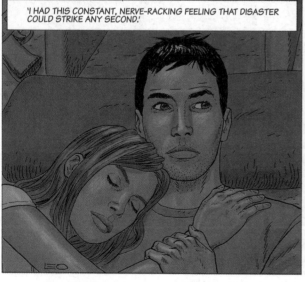

'I HAD THIS CONSTANT, NERVE-RACKING FEELING THAT DISASTER COULD STRIKE ANY SECOND.'

'IT WASN'T UNTIL THE SMALL HOURS OF THE MORNING THAT EXHAUSTION WON OUT AND I NODDED OFF.'

38

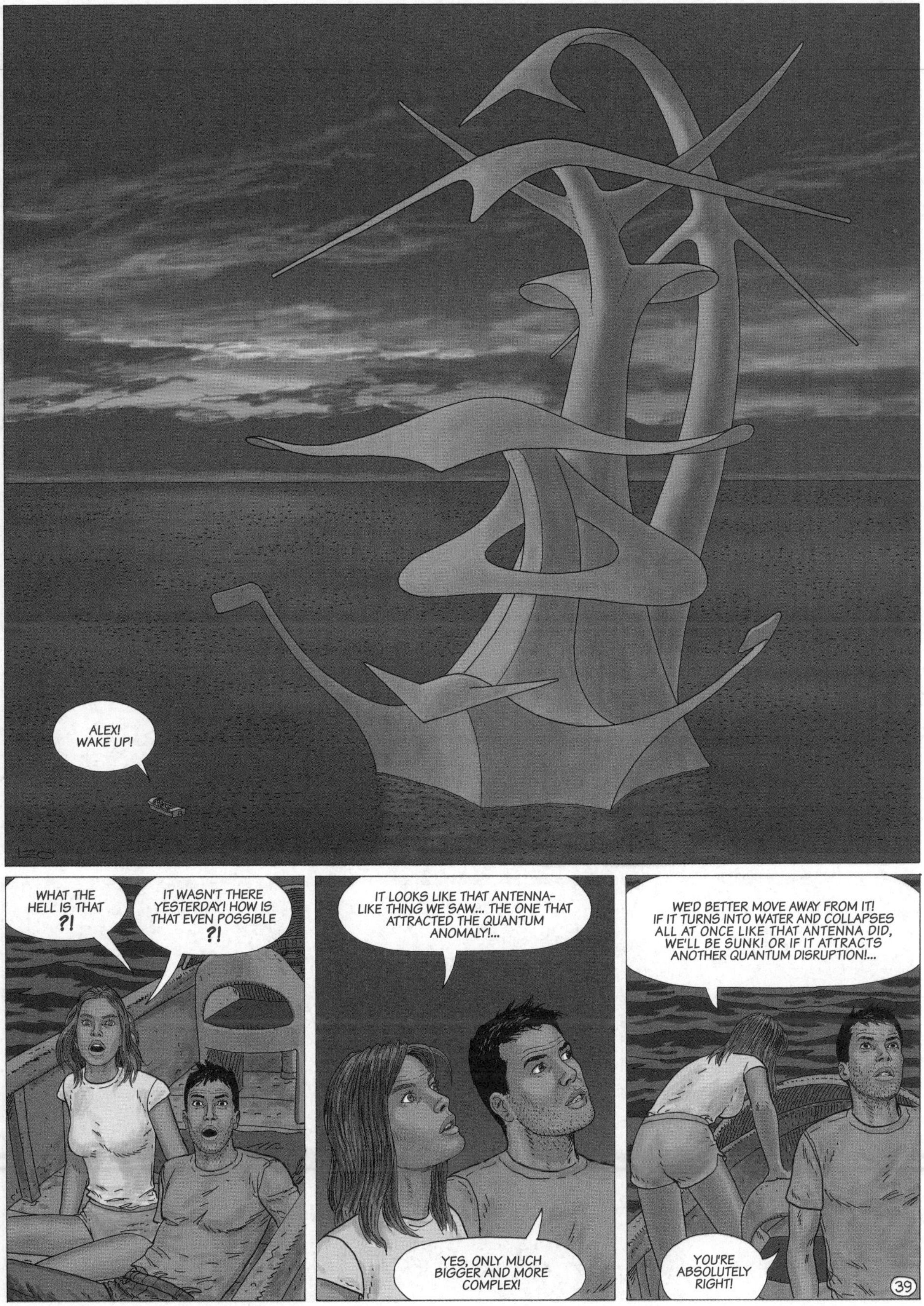
ALEX! WAKE UP!
WHAT THE HELL IS THAT ?!
IT WASN'T THERE YESTERDAY! HOW IS THAT EVEN POSSIBLE ?!
IT LOOKS LIKE THAT ANTENNA-LIKE THING WE SAW... THE ONE THAT ATTRACTED THE QUANTUM ANOMALY!...
YES, ONLY MUCH BIGGER AND MORE COMPLEX!
WE'D BETTER MOVE AWAY FROM IT! IF IT TURNS INTO WATER AND COLLAPSES ALL AT ONCE LIKE THAT ANTENNA DID, WE'LL BE SUNK! OR IF IT ATTRACTS ANOTHER QUANTUM DISRUPTION!...
YOU'RE ABSOLUTELY RIGHT!
39

HEY! LOOK!

WHAT THE...?!

'SWIFTLY, A WALL OF WATER SURROUNDED US...'

'...BEFORE CLOSING OVER OUR HEADS, ESSENTIALLY CONFINING US INSIDE A SORT OF SEAWATER BUBBLE.'

'INSTINCTIVELY, MARIE AND I HELD ON TIGHT TO EACH OTHER. YET I WASN'T AFRAID. I FELT STRANGELY SERENE. TOO MUCH SO...'

'...TO THE POINT THAT WHEN THOSE EXTRUSIONS BEGAN TO GROW TOWARDS US, TOWARDS OUR FACES, I DIDN'T MOVE BACK!'

'ON THEIR EXTREMITIES THEY HELD A BLUE CAPSULE AND, WITHOUT EVEN PAUSING TO CONSIDER THE RECKLESSNESS OF OUR ACTS, WE SWALLOWED THEM.'

ALEX! WHAT DID WE JUST DO?! WE ATE THOSE THINGS!

IT... IT'S CRAZY!... BUT I FEEL STRANGELY GOOD, CALM... DON'T YOU?

YES, IT'S TRUE... I FEEL GOOD TOO... I FEEL ... HAPPY!

'THE WATER BUBBLE SOON DISAPPEARED, FREEING OUR BOAT. WE IMMEDIATELY DECIDED TO PUT SOME DISTANCE BETWEEN US AND THAT... THAT THING.'

'BUT I COULDN'T STOP TURNING BACK AGAIN AND AGAIN TO STARE AT THE PREPOSTEROUS STRUCTURE. I WAS FILLED WITH DEEP AND BAFFLING EMOTION.'

40

'OUR SECOND DAY AT SEA WAS UNEVENTFUL, BUT AS EVENING DREW TO A CLOSE, STRONG RAIN BEGAN TO LASH AT US, AND THE SEA BECAME DISTINCTLY THREATENING!'

'CAPSIZING IN THIS WEATHER WOULD MEAN DEATH. MARIE PERFORMED MIRACLE AFTER MIRACLE TO KEEP OUR BOW TURNED TOWARD THE ENORMOUS WAVES!'

'WITH THE MORNING, EVERYTHING TURNED QUIET AS IF BY MAGIC, AND THE SUN CAME BACK. WE WERE EXHAUSTED, BUT WE WERE ALIVE.'

'I'D TAKEN THE HELM TO ALLOW MARIE TO SLEEP AFTER HER EFFORTS OF THE NIGHT. THAT WAS WHEN THE NEXT ROUND OF SURPRISES AND WEIRD STUFF BEGAN...'

'FIRST I FELT A DISTINCT LOSS OF POWER, AND THE BOAT SLOWED DOWN. I THOUGHT THAT THE BATTERIES MUST BE NEARING THE END OF THEIR CHARGE AFTER TWO LONG DAYS OF HEAVY USE.'

'THEN THERE WAS A STRANGE SCENE: A HUGE FISH JUMPED OUT OF THE WATER...'

'...BUT UPON FALLING BACK, IT STAYED ON THE SURFACE, NOT SINKING, IN A CLEARLY UNNATURAL WAY!'

'THEN, INCREDULOUS, SHOCKED, I UNDERSTOOD...'

MARIE!

WHAT IS IT?!

THE WATER! I KNOW IT'S RIDICULOUS, BUT IT'S TURNING INTO JELLY!

WHAT!?

LOOK!

WHOA!

THE THING IS, THE BOAT IS STUCK NOW!

THE WATER IS BECOMING INCREASINGLY SOLID! IT'S ALMOST LIKE RUBBER AT THIS POINT!

ALEX! THE FISH!...

SHIT! IT'S AS IF THE SEA IS COMING TO LIFE! IT'S GOING TO SWALLOW THAT FISH!

I DON'T LIKE THIS. I DON'T LIKE THIS AT ALL!

HEY! IT'S COMING AFTER OUR BOAT NOW!

WHAT DO WE DO?!

OVER THERE! LOOK!

42

44

THE COAST!

I DIDN'T EVEN SEE IT!

YOU KNOW WHAT WE HAVE TO DO, DON'T YOU?

WHAT?

WE'RE GOING TO HAVE TO WALK TO THE SHORE. THOSE TENDRILS TAKE SOME TIME FORMING. IF WE DON'T STOP, THEY WON'T BE ABLE TO TRAP US.

YOU THINK SO?...

NOT LIKE WE HAVE A CHOICE. LOOK WHAT'S HAPPENING TO THE FISH!

IT WON'T BE LONG BEFORE THE BOAT'S BURIED — AND US WITH IT IF WE JUST STAND HERE!

THE OCEAN TURNING SOLID! IT'S COMPLETELY INSANE!

AFTER OUR JUMPS INTO THE FUTURE, NOTHING ABOUT THIS PLANET CAN SURPRISE ME.

'RUNNING ON THAT UNEVEN, RUBBERY SURFACE WAS FAR FROM EASY!'

'WHAT WAS MORE, THE SOLIDIFICATION PHENOMENON GAVE OFF HEAT. COMBINED WITH THE ALREADY SCORCHING SUN, IT WAS EXCRUCIATING!'

43

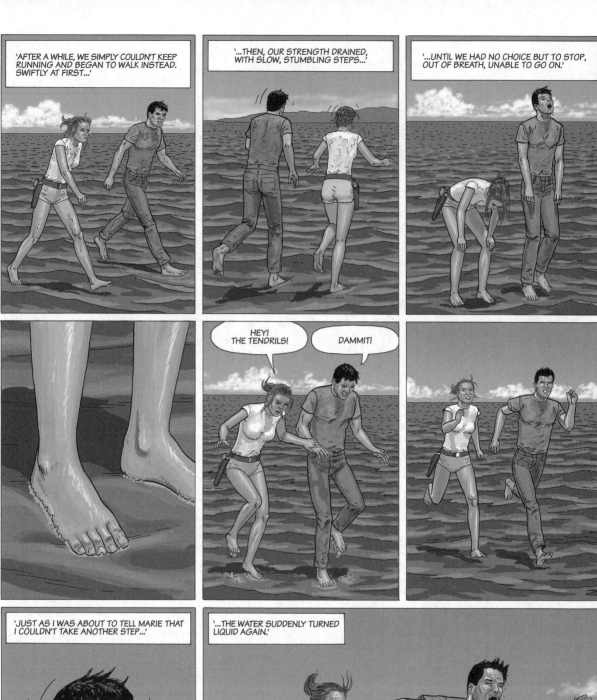

'AFTER A WHILE, WE SIMPLY COULDN'T KEEP RUNNING AND BEGAN TO WALK INSTEAD. SWIFTLY AT FIRST...'

'...THEN, OUR STRENGTH DRAINED, WITH SLOW, STUMBLING STEPS...'

'...UNTIL WE HAD NO CHOICE BUT TO STOP, OUT OF BREATH, UNABLE TO GO ON.'

HEY! THE TENDRILS!

DAMMIT!

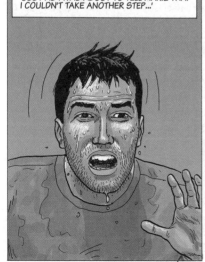

'JUST AS I WAS ABOUT TO TELL MARIE THAT I COULDN'T TAKE ANOTHER STEP...'

'...THE WATER SUDDENLY TURNED LIQUID AGAIN.'

44

46

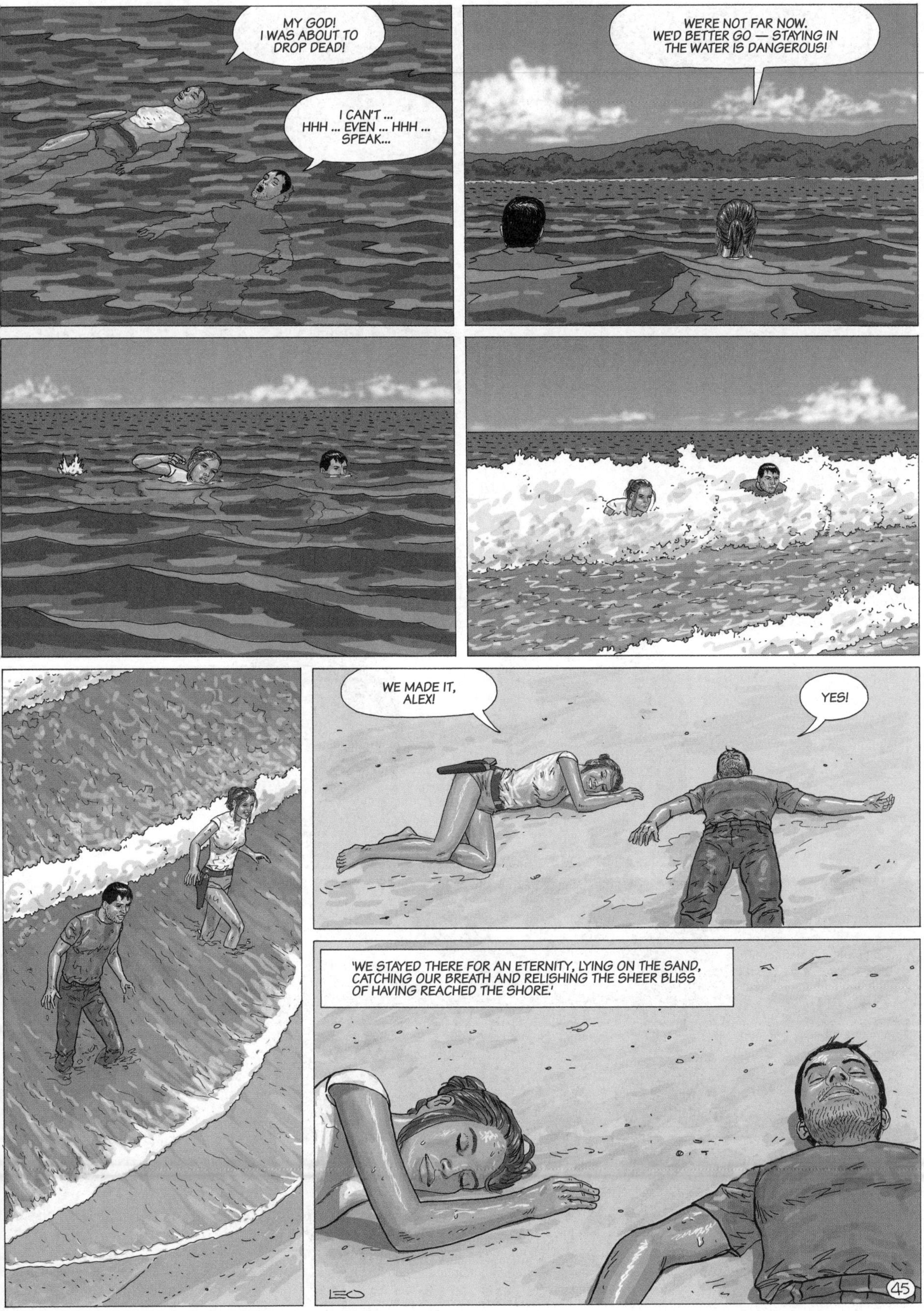
MY GOD! I WAS ABOUT TO DROP DEAD!
I CAN'T ... HHH ... EVEN ... HHH ... SPEAK...
WE'RE NOT FAR NOW. WE'D BETTER GO — STAYING IN THE WATER IS DANGEROUS!
WE MADE IT, ALEX!
YES!
'WE STAYED THERE FOR AN ETERNITY, LYING ON THE SAND, CATCHING OUR BREATH AND RELISHING THE SHEER BLISS OF HAVING REACHED THE SHORE.'
LEO
45

RIGHT...
OUR CROSSING WAS
SUCCESSFUL, BUT IT WAS
ONLY THE FIRST
STEP...

YES... WE NEED
TO FIND WATER AND
A SHELTER FOR THE
NIGHT.

WHICH DIRECTION
SHALL WE TAKE?

HOW ABOUT
THIS WAY?

SCRIPT,
ARTWORK,
COLOURS

LEO
2015

46

TO BE CONTINUED...